MW00711178

# The BS Joke Book of One Liners, Jokes & Puns

Burhan Siddiqui

To the class of 8B 2012 – 2013 and Mr. Brown who inspired
and motivated me to write this book.

# Q & A

# Jokes

What do you call a sleeping bull?
A bull-dozer.

What is the loudest pet?
The trum-pet.

What did the farmer call the cow that had
no milk?
An udder failure.

Why do gorillas have big nostrils?
Because they have big fingers!

What do you get from a pampered cow?
Spoiled milk.

Why are teddy bears never hungry?
They are always stuffed!

Why do fish live in salt water?
Because pepper makes them sneeze!

Where do polar bears vote?
The North Poll

What did the judge say when the skunk
walked in the courtroom?
Odor in the court!

What sound do porcupines make when they
kiss?
Ouch!

Why did the snake cross the road?
To get to the other ssssssside!

Why are fish so smart?
Because they live in schools.

What do you call a cow that won't give milk?
A milk dud!

What's grey and has a trunk?
A mouse on vacation.

How does a lion greet the other animals in
the field?
Pleased to eat you.

Burhan Siddiqui

What happened when the lion ate the
comedian?
He felt funny!

What fish only swims at night?
A starfish!

Why is a fish easy to weigh?
Because it has its own scales!

What do you get when a chicken lays an egg
on top of a barn?
An eggroll!

Why didn't the chicken cross the road?
Because there was a KFC on the
other side!

Why did the chicken cross the road?
To show everyone he wasn't chicken!

What do you call a sick alligator?
An ill-igator.

What's a reptile's favorite movie?
The Lizard of Oz.

What animals are on legal documents?
Seals!

What do you get when you cross a snake
and a pie?
A pie-thon!

What is "out of bounds?"
An exhausted kangaroo!

What did the buffalo say to his son when he
went away on a trip?
Bison!

Why didn't the boy believe the tiger?
He thought it was a lion!

How do bees get to school?
By school buzz!

What do you call a bear with no ears?
B!

What animal has more lives than a cat?
Frogs, they croak every night!

What do you give a sick bird?
Tweetment!

What is black and white and black and white
and black and white and?
A penguin falling down the stairs!

When does a teacher carry birdseed?
When there is a parrot-teacher
conference!

Why is there a fence around the cemetery?
Because people are dying to get in!

What kind of bird works at a construction
site?
The crane!

Why does a flamingo lift up one leg?
Because if it lifted both legs it would
fall over!

Why do students always do so poorly after
Thanksgiving?
Because everything gets marked
down after the holidays!

What did the sick chicken say?
Oh no! I have the people-pox!

What do you call a funny chicken?
A comedi-hen

Why do scientists think humming birds hum?
Because they can't remember the words!

What bird is always depressed?
The blue jay

Why do seagulls like to live by the sea?
Because if they lived by the bay they would be bagels!

What is a cat's favorite color?
Purrr-ple

Why are ghosts' bad liars?
Because you can see right through them.

What's worse than raining cats and dogs?
Hailing taxis!

Why are cats good at video games?
Because they have nine lives!

Why did the invisible man turn down the job?
He just couldn't see himself doing it.

What song does a cat like best?
Three Blind Mice.

What game did the cat like to play with the mouse?
Catch!

Where did the school kittens go for their field trip?
To the mewseum

Why did the cat go to medical school?
To become a first aid kit

Who was the first cat to fly in an airplane?
Kitty-hawk

What dinosaur would Harry Potter be?
The Dinosorcerer

Have you ever seen a catfish?
No. How could he hold the rod and reel?

What state has a lot of cats and dogs?
Petsylvania

What do you call a dinosaur with no eyes?
Doyouthinkysaraus

What do you call a sleeping dinosaur?
A dino-snore!

How do you know if there is a dinosaur in your refrigerator?
The door won't shut!

How can you best raise a baby dinosaur?
With a crane!

What did the dinosaur put on her steak?
Dinosauce

What came after the dinosaur?
It's tail!

Why was the Stegosaurus such a good
volleyball player?
Because he could really spike the
ball!

What does a triceratops sit on?
Its tricera-bottom.

What do dinosaurs use on the floors of their
kitchens?
Rep-tiles

What is the best thing to do if you see a
Tyrannosaurus Rex?
Hope that it doesn't see you.

What's the nickname for someone who put
their right hand in the mouth of a T-Rex?
Lefty

What do you get when you cross a turtle
and a porcupine?
A slow-poke.

What dog keeps the best time?
A watch dog!

Why did the dinosaur cross the road?
To eat the chickens on the other side.

What do you call a paleontologist who sleeps all the time?
Lazy bones

What do you get when a dinosaur scores a touchdown?
A dino-score

What did the dinosaur use to build his house?
A dino-saw

Why don't blind people like to sky dive?
Because it scares the dog!

Why did the poor dog chase his own tail?
He was trying to make both ends meet!

Why don't dogs make good dancers?
Because they have two left feet!

What happens when it rains cats and dogs?
You can step in a poodle!

Why are dogs like phones?
Because they have collar IDs.

How does the teacher read schoolwork?
With her pupils

What did the dog say when he sat on
sandpaper?
Ruff!

What do you call a dog that is left handed?
A south paw!

What did one flea say to the other?
Should we walk or take a dog?

What type of markets do dogs avoid?
Flea markets!

What did the cowboy say when his dog ran
away?
Well, doggone!

What time does a duck wake up?
At the quack of dawn!

What do ducks get after they eat?
A bill!

Why do geese make bad drivers?
All they do it honk

Who stole the soap?
The robber ducky!

What do you get if you cross fireworks with
a duck?
A firequacker!

What has fangs and webbed feet?
Count Duckula

What was the goal of the detective duck?
To quack the case

Why was the duck put into the basketball
game?
To make a fowl shot!

What did the duck do after he read all these jokes?
He quacked up!

What time is it when an elephant sits on the fence?
Time to fix the fence!

Why did the elephant sit on the marshmallow?
So he wouldn't fall into the hot chocolate.

Why are elephants so wrinkled?
Did you ever try to iron one?

What would you do if an elephant sat in front of you at a movie?
Miss most of the film.

What do you do when you see an elephant with a basketball?
Get out of its way!

What is gray and blue and very big?
An elephant holding its breath!

What time is it when ten elephants are chasing you?
Ten after one!

What wears glass slippers and weighs over 4,000 pounds?
Cinderellephant

What was the elephant's favorite sport?
Squash

What should you know if you want to be a lion tamer?
More than the lion

How do you keep a rhino from charging?
You take off the charging cable!

What do you do with a blue elephant?
You try and cheer her up

A man rode his horse to town on Friday. The next day he rode back on Friday. How is this possible?
The horse's name was Friday.

Why did the pony have to gargle?
Because it was a little horse!

What did the horse say when it fell?
I've fallen and I can't giddy up!

What did the teacher say when the horse
walked into the class?
Why the long face?

What do you call a horse that lives next
door?
A neigh-bor!

When does a horse talk?
Whinney wants to!

What's the best way to lead a horse to
water?
With lots of apples and carrots!

How long should a horse's legs be?
Long enough to reach the ground

Which side of the horse has the most hair?
The outside!

Why did the man stand behind the horse?
He was hoping to get a kick out of
it

How do rabbits travel?
By hareplane.

What is a bunny's motto?
Don't be mad, be hoppy!

How do you catch a unique rabbit?
Unique up on it.

How do you know carrots are good for your
eyes?
Because you never see rabbits
wearing glasses!

What is a rabbit's favorite dance style?
Hip-Hop!

Where do rabbits go after their wedding?
On their bunnymoon!

What does a baby computer call his father?
Data!

What do you get if you cross a rabbit with an insect?
Bugs bunny

What disease was the horse scared of getting?
Hay fever!

What do you call a group of rabbits hopping backwards?
A receding hare line

What do you call a rabbit who is angry over gettting burnt?
A hot cross bunny

How can you tell which rabbits are getting old?
Look for the grey hares

Why are rabbits so lucky?
They have four rabbit's feet?

What did the spider do on the computer?
Made a website!

What did the computer do at lunchtime?
Had a byte!

Why did the computer keep sneezing?
It had a virus!

What is a computer virus?
A terminal illness!

Why was the computer cold?
It left its Windows open!

Why was there a bug in the computer?
Because it was looking for a byte to
eat?

Why did the computer squeak?
Because someone stepped on its
mouse!

"Waiter, this food tastes kind of funny?"
"Then why aren't you laughing?"

Where do all the cool mice live?
In their mouse pads

What do you get when you cross a computer with an elephant?
Lots of memory!

What is black; white; green and bumpy?
A pickle wearing a tuxedo.

What do you call cheese that isn't yours?
Nacho cheese!

What kind of coffee was served on the Titanic?
Sanka!

What's the best thing to put into a pie?
Your teeth!

What do you get when you cross a computer and a life guard?
A screensaver!

Did you hear the joke about the peanut butter?
I'm not telling you. You might spread it!

Why do the French like to eat snails?
Because they don't like fast food!

Why shouldn't you tell an egg a joke?
Because it might crack up!

What did the baby corn say to it's mom?
Where is pop corn?

What do you call candy that was stolen?
Hot chocolate!

What kind of nuts always seems to have a
cold?
Cashews!

"Waiter, will my pizza be long?"
"No sir, it will be round!"

What is green and sings?
Elvis Parsley

Why did the banana go to the doctor?
Because it wasn't peeling well!

What is white, has a horn, and gives milk?
A dairy truck!

What candy do you eat on the playground?
Recess pieces.

Why did the fisherman put peanut butter
into the sea?
To go with the jellyfish!

Why don't you starve in a desert?
Because of all the 'sand which is' there.

What do you call a snail on a ship?
A snailer.

In which school do you learn to make ice
cream?
Sundae School.

What do elves make sandwiches with?
Shortbread

Why shouldn't you tell a secret on a farm?
Because the potatoes have eyes and
the corn has ears.

What is a pretzel's favorite dance?
The Twist!

What are twins favorite fruit?
Pears!

What do you give to a sick lemon?
Lemon aid!

Why did the lady love to drink hot chocolate?
Because she was a cocoanut!

How do you make a milk shake?
Give it a good scare!

What do you call a peanut in a spacesuit?
An astronut!

What kind of keys do kids like to carry?
Cookies!

Why don't they serve chocolate in prison?
Because it makes you break out!

What cheese is made backwards?
Edam.

What is a cow's favorite day?
Moo-years Day!

What do you get a man who has everything
for his birthday?
A burglar alarm!

What do you get when you plant kisses?
Two lips.

What did the light bulb say to her man on
Valentine's Day?
I wuv you watts and watts.

Where do bunnies get their breakfast?
IHOP!

How does the Easter bunny stay in shape?
Lots of eggercise!

What was the most popular dance in 1776?
Indepen-dance!

What do you call a fake stone in Ireland?
A sham rock

Why is St. Patrick's day most frog's favorite holiday?
Because they are already wearing green

What do you get when you cross a snowman with a vampire?
Frostbite.

Why does Santa Claus like to go down the chimney?
Because it soots him!

What do Santa's elves do after school?
Their gnomework!

What do snowmen like to eat for breakfast?
Frosted Flakes!

What is a parent's favorite Christmas carol?
Silent Night.

What is the fear of Santa Claus called?
Claustrophobia

What nationality is Santa Claus?
North Polish!

What does Tarzan sing and Christmas?
Jungle Bells!

Why does Santa have a field?
So he can hoe, hoe, hoe!

Why is it cold on Christmas?
Because it's in Decembrrrrrrrr!

How did they send the turkey through the mail?
Bird class!

What happened when the turkey got into a fight?
He got the stuffing knocked out of him!

What do you call a single vampire?
A bat-chelor.

What did the bat say to his valentine?
I love hanging around you.

Who was the drumer in the Thanksgiving band?
The turkey, because he had the drumsticks!

What type of key is not good for opening doors?
A Tur-key!

What kind of car did the Pilgrim drive?
A Plymouth

Why should you never set the turkey next to the desert?
Because he will gobble, gobble it up!

What always comes at the end of Thanksgiving?
The G

Why didn't the skeleton cross the road?
He didn't have the guts!

Why are graveyards noisy?
Because of all the coffin!

Why did the dog hand up his stocking at Christmas?
He was waiting for Santa Paws.

When is it bad luck to meet a black cat?
When you are a mouse.

What is a scarecrows favorite fruit?
Straw-berries!

What did the boy ghost say to the girl ghost?
You sure are Boo-tiful!

Why was the baby ghost sad?
He wanted his mummy!

What do witches put on their bagels?
Scream Cheese

Why are vampires tough to get along with?
Because they can be pains in the neck!

Do you know how to make a witch itch?
You take away the w!

What subject in school is easy for a witch?
Spell-ing

Why did Mozart get rid of his chickens?
They kept saying Bach, Bach!

Why couldn't the athlete listen to her music?
Because she broke the record!

What type of music are balloons scared of?
Pop music!

What makes music on your head?
A head band!

What part of the turkey is musical?
The drumstick!

What has forty feet and sings?
The school choir!

Why did the girl sit on the ladder to sing?
She wanted to reach the high notes!

What is the musical part of a snake?
The scales!

What do you call a cow that can play a musical instrument?
A moo-sician

What makes pirates such good singers?
They can hit the high Cs!

How can you tell the ocean is friendly?
It waves.

What kind of hair do oceans have?
Wavy!

What did Mars say to Saturn?
Give me a ring sometime.

What is the difference between a fish and a piano?
You can't tuna fish!

Where does seaweed go to look for a job?
The kelp wanted section.

When is the moon the heaviest?
When it's full!

What type of songs do the planets sing?
Nep-tunes!

What kind of flower grows on your face?
Tulips!

What washes up on very small beaches?
Microwaves!

What do you call an attractive volcano?
Lava-ble!

What did the tornado say to the sports car?
Want to go for a spin!

What kind of shorts to clouds wear?
Thunderwear!

What's a tornado's favorite game?
Twister!

What is the opposite of a cold front?
A warm back

What bow can't be tied?
A rainbow!

What falls but never hits the ground?
The temperature!

How do hurricanes see?
With one eye!

What did the cloud say to the lightning bolt?
You're shocking!

What happens when the fog disperses in
California?
UCLA!

How hot is it?
It's so hot, when I turned on my
lawn sprinkler, all I got was steam!

Who does everyone listen to, but no one
believes?
The weatherman

What did the tree wear to the pool party?
Swimming trunks!

What did the beaver say to the tree?
It's been nice gnawing you!

Why did the leaf go to the doctor?
It was feeling green!

What is a tree's least favorite month?
Sep-timber!

What kind of tree can fit into your hand?
A palm tree!

How do trees get on the internet?
They log in.

What did the little tree say to the big tree?
Leaf me alone!

Did you hear the one about the oak tree?
It's a corn-y one!

What did the lawyer name his daughter?
Sue

Why did the shoelace get into trouble?
Because it was being knotty

What did the tree do when the bank closed?
It started a new branch

What do you call an underwater spy?
James Pond!

Why did the policeman go to the baseball game?
He heard someone had stolen a base!

Why did the book join the police?
He wanted to go undercover!

Why was there thunder and lightning in the lab?
The scientists were brainstorming!

What do lawyers wear to court?
Lawsuits!

What kind of card does a farmer drive?
A cornvertable!

What do you call a flying police officer?
A helicopper!

How did the farmer mend his pants?
With cabbage patches!

Why did the lazy man want a job in a bakery?
So he could loaf around!

Why did the farmer ride his horse to town?
It was too heavy to carry!

What do you call a happy cowboy?
A jolly rancher.

What did one tooth say to the other tooth?
Thar's gold in them fills!

What did the judge say to the dentist?
Do you swear to pull the tooth, the whole tooth and nothing but the tooth?

Why did the tree go to the dentist?
To get a root canal.

Why did the king go to the dentist?
To get his teeth crowned!

What time do you go to the dentist?
Tooth-Hurty!

What does a dentist do during an earthquake?
She braces herself!

What did the tooth say to the dentist as she was leaving?
Fill me in when you get back

What is a dentist's favorite animal?
A molar bear!

How can you tell that a tree is a dogwood tree?
By its bark!

Has your tooth stopped hurting yet?
I don't know, the dentist kept it.

What did the dentist get for an award?
A little plaque

When does a doctor get mad?
When he runs out of patients!

Why did the pillow go to the doctor?
He was feeling all stuffed up!

Why did the doctor lose his temper?
Because he didn't have any patients!

Where does a boat go when it's sick?
To the dock!

What did on tonsil say to the other tonsil?
Get dressed up, the doctor is taking
us out!

Patient: Doctor, sometimes I feel like I'm
invisible.
Doctor: Who said that?

What gets wetter the more it dries?
A towel.

Patient: Doctor, Doctor I think I'm a moth.
Doctor: Get out of my light!

What do you call a boy named Lee that no
one talks to?
Lonely

What do you call a snake that works?
A boa-constructor.

What did one tonsil say to the other tonsil?
I hear the doctor is taking us out
tonight!

Did you hear the one about the germ?
Never mind, I don't want to spread
it around

Why did the cookie go to the hospital?
He was feeling really crumbie!

What goes up and down but does not move?
Stairs

Where should a 500 pound alien go?
On a diet

What did one toilet say to the other?
You look a bit flushed.

Why did the picture go to jail?
Because it was framed.

What did one wall say to the other wall?
I'll meet you at the corner.

What did the paper say to the pencil?
Write on!

Why do bicycles fall over?
Because they are two-tired!

Why do dragons sleep during the day?
So they can fight knights!

What did Cinderella say when her photos did
not show up?
Someday my prints will come!

Why was the broom late?
It over swept!

What part of the car is the laziest?
The wheels, because they are always
tired!

What did the stamp say to the envelope?
Stick with me and we will go places!

When do kangaroos celebrate their birthdays?
On a leap year!

How long were you in the hospital?
I was the same size I am now!

Why couldn't the pirate play cards?
Because he was sitting on the deck!

What did the laundryman say to the
impatient customer?
Keep your shirt on!

What's the difference between a TV and a
newspaper?
Ever tried swatting a fly with a TV?

What did one elevator say to the other
elevator?
I think I'm coming down with
something!

Why was the belt arrested?
Because it held up some pants!

Why was everyone so tired on April 1st?
They had just finished a March of
31 days.

Which hand is it better to write with?
Neither, it's best to write with a pen!

What makes the calendar seem so popular?
Because it has a lot of dates!

Why did Mickey Mouse take a trip into space?
He wanted to find Pluto!

What is it that even the most careful person overlooks?
Her nose!

Did you hear about the robbery last night?
Two clothespins held up a pair of pants!

Why do you go to bed every night?
Because the bed won't come to you!

Who isn't hungry on Thanksgiving?
The turkey, because he's already stuffed!

How do you cure a hadache?
Put your head through a window and the pane will just disappear!

What has four wheels and flies?
A garbage truck!

What kind of car does Mickey Mouse's wife drive?
A minnie van!

Why don't traffic lights ever go swimming?
Because they take too long to change!

Why did the robber take a bath before he stole from the bank?
He wanted to make a clean get away!

What has one head, one foot and four legs?
A Bed

Did you hear the joke about the roof?
Never mind, it's over your head!

How many letters are in The Alphabet?
There are 11 letters in "The Alphabet."

How can you spell freezing with two letters?
IC!

Why did the man run around his bed?
To catch up on his sleep!

Which president was least guilty?
Lincoln. He is in a cent.

David's father had three sons: Snap, Crackle, and…?
David!

If you were in a race and passed the person in 2nd place, what place would you be in?
2nd place!

What is the center of gravity?
The letter V!

Alvin: Doctor, I keep hearing a ringing sound.
Doctor: Then answer the phone!

Why did pilgrims' pants always fall down?
Because they wore their belt buckle
on their hat!

What has a head, a tail, is brown, and has no
legs?
A penny!

What gets bigger and bigger as you take
more away from it?
A hole!

How many months have 28 days?
All of them!

Can you spell rotted with two letters?
DK!

How many books can you put into an empty
backpack?
One! After that it's not empty.

Which weighs more, a ton of feathers or a
ton of bricks?
Neither, they both weigh a ton!

Does your shirt have holes in it?
No, then how did you put it on?

What starts with a P and ends with an E
and has a million letters in it?
Post Office!

What goes up, but never comes down?
Your age!

When does a cart come before a horse?
In the dictionary!

What is full of holes but can still hold water?
A sponge!

What has two hands, a round face, always
runs, but stays in place?
A clock!

Where does success come before work?
In the dictionary!

Why did Billy go out with a prune?
Because he couldn't find a date!

What breaks when you say it?
Silence!

How many peas are there in a pint?
There is one 'P' in a 'pint'.

What did the ground say to the earthquake?
You crack me up!

Why did the music teacher need a ladder?
To reach the high notes.

What's the worst thing you're likely to find in
the school cafeteria?
The Food!

What kind of plates do they use on Venus?
Flying saucers!

Why did nose not want to go to school?
He was tired of getting picked on!

How do you get straight A's?
By using a ruler!

What did the pen say to the pencil?
So, what's your point!

How did the music teacher get locked in the classroom?
His keys were inside the piano!

What do elves learn in school?
The elf-abet!

What did you learn in school today?
Not enough, I have to go back tomorrow!

What holds the sun up in the sky?
Sunbeams!

What object is king of the classroom?
The ruler!
When do astronauts eat?
At launch time!

What did the pencil sharpener say to the pencil?
Stop going in circles and get to the point!

How does the barber cut the moon's hair?
E-clipse it!

What happened when the wheel was invented?
It caused a revolution!

What do librarians take with them when they go fishing?
Bookworms

What is the world's tallest building?
The library because it has the most stories.

What vegetables to librarians like?
Quiet peas.

Why did the clock in the cafeteria run slow?
It always went back four seconds.

Why didn't the sun go to college?
Because it already had a million degrees!

What has 5 eyes and is lying on the water?
The Mississippi River

Where do the pianists go for vacation?
Florida Keys

What is the smartest state?
Alabama, it has four A's and one B.

What stays in the corner, but travels around
the world?
A stamp!

Where to pencils come from?
Pennsylvania!

What are the Great Plains?
The 747, Concorde and F-16!

What is the capital of Alaska?
Come on, Juneau this one!

What rock group has four men that don't
sing?
Mount Rushmore!

What city cheats at exams?
Peking!

What is the capital of Washington?
The W!

What did Delaware?
Her New Jersey!

What is the fastest country in the world?
Rush-a!

Teacher: What can you tell me about the
Dead Sea?
Student: I didn't even know it was sick!

Why were the early days of history called
the dark ages?
Because there were so many knights!

Why is England the wettest country?
Because the queen has reigned there
for years!

How did the Vikings send secret messages?
By norse code!

Who invented fractions?
Henry the 1/4th!

What kind of lighting did Noah use for the ark?
Floodlights!

What did they do at the Boston Tea Party?
I don't know, I wasn't invited!

What's purple and 5000 miles long?
The grape wall of China.

What did Mason say to Dixon?
We've got to draw the line here!

Who made King Arthur's round table?
Sir-Cumference

Who built the ark?
I have Noah idea!

"Why aren't you doing well in history?"
"Because the teacher keeps on asking about things that happened before I was born!"

What did Ceasar say to Cleopatra?
Toga-ether we can rule the world!

Where was the Declaration of Independence
signed?
At the bottom!

What do Alexander the Great and Kermit the
Frog have in common?
The same middle name!

What is the fruitiest subject at school?
History, because it's full of dates!

Why did the pioneers cross the country in
covered wagons?
Because they didn't want to wait 40
years for a train!

When a knight was killed in battle, what sign
did they put on his grave?
Rust in peace!

How was the Roman Empire cut in half?
With a pair of Caesars!

Why didn't the quarter roll down the hill with the nickel?
Because it had more cents.

What kind of meals do math teachers eat?
Square meals!

Why didn't the two 4's want any dinner?
Because they already 8!

What is a math teacher's favorite sum?
Summer!

How is an English teacher like a judge?
They both give out sentences.

What do you get when you divide the circumference of a Jack-o-lantern by its diameter?
Pumpkin Pi!

What did zero say to the number eight?
Nice belt.

What do camels wear to hide themselves?
Camel-flauge.

**Teacher:** Why are you doing your multiplication on the floor?
**Student:** You told me not to use tables.

Why did the teacher wear sunglasses?
Because his class was so bright!

What is a ghosts favorite position in soccer?
Ghoul keeper.

Why were the teacher's eyes crossed?
She couldn't control her pupils!

Why did the teacher go to the beach?
To test the water.

What is a cheerleaders favorite color?
Yeller!
Why did closing her eyes remind the teacher of her classroom?
Because there were no pupils to see.

What do you do if a teacher rolls her eyes at you?
Pick them up and roll them back

What did the ghost teacher say to the class?
Look at the board and I will go through it again.

Why did the teacher write on the window?
Because she wanted the lesson to be very clear!

What do you call four bullfighters in quicksand?
Quattro sinko.

What do you call a boomerang that doesn't work?
A stick.

What's a golfer's favorite letter?
Tee!
Why couldn't the student stand at the end of the line?
There was already someone there.

What is a butterfly's favorite subject at school?
Mothematics.

Why can't Cinderella play soccer?
Because she's always running away
from the ball.

When is a baby good at basketball?
When it's dribbling!

Why did the basketball player go to jail?
Because he shot the ball.

Why do basketball players love donuts?
Because they dunk them!

What do you call a pig who plays basketball?
A ball hog!

Why did the golfer wear two pairs of pants?
In case he got a hole in one!

How is a baseball team similar to a pancake?
They both need a good batter!

What animal is best at hitting a baseball?
A bat!

At what sport to waiters do really well?
Tennis, because they can serve so well.

How do baseball players stay cool?
They sit next to the fans!

Why did the football coach go to the bank?
He wanted his quarter back!

What is harder to catch the faster you run?
Your breath!

Why is tennis such a loud sport?
The players raise a racquet.

Why did Tarzan spend so much time on the golf course?
He was perfecting his swing.

Why did the ballerina quit?
Because it was tu-tu hard!

How do football players stay cool during the game?
They stand close to the fans?

What is an insect's favorite sport?
Cricket!

What do hockey players and magicians have
in common?
Both do hat tricks!

Why did the man keep doing the backstroke?
Because he just ate and didn't want
to swim on a full stomach!

What is the hardest part about skydiving?
The ground!

Why did Krisha get fired from the hotdog
stand?
She put her hair in a bun!

Where do ants go for their holidays?
Frants!

What is a Cheerleader's favorite food?
Cheerios!

What do you call an ant who skips school?
A truant!

What do you get if youcross some ants with some tics?
All sorts of antics!

What do you call a greedy ant?
An anteater!

Why did the elephant put his trunk across the path?
To trip up the ants!

What is even bigger than an elephant?
A giant!

What do you call an ant in space?
Cosmonants & Astronants!

What do you call an ant from overseas?
Impartant!

What medicine would you give an ill ant?
Antibiotics!

What kind of money to polo bears use?
Ice lolly!

Have you ever hunted bear?
No, but I've been shooting in my shorts!

How do you start a teddy bear race?
Ready, teddy, go!

Why do bears have fur coats?
Because they'd look stupid in anoraks!

What do you get if you cross a teddy bear with a pig?
A teddy boar!

What should you call a bald teddy?
Fred bear!

How do you hire a teddy bear?
Put him on stilts!

What animal do you look like when you get into the bath?
A little bear!

What do you get if you cross a skunk with a bear?
Winnie the Pooh!

What do you get if you cross a grizzly bear and a harp?
A bear faced lyre!

What do you call a big white bear with a hole in his middle?
A polo bear!

What do you call a very rude bird?
A mockingbird!

What is a polygon?
A dead parrot!

Why do polo bears like bald men?
Because they have a great, white, bear place!

What do polo bears have for lunch?
Ice burger!

What's a teddy bears favorite pasta?
Tagliateddy!

What do Alexander the Great and Winnie the Pooh have in common?
They both have 'the' as their middle names!

Why is polar bear cheap to have as a pet?
It lives on ice!

Why shouldn't you take a bear to the zoo?
Because they'd rather go to the cinema!

Why was the little bear so spoiled?
Because its mother panda'd to its every whim!

What flies through the jungle singing opera?
The parrots of Penzance!

What do you get if you cross a duck with a firework?
A firequaker!

What is a parrot's favorite game?
Hide and Speak!

Why did the parrot wear a raincoat?
Because she wanted to be a Polly
unsaturated!

What did the gamekeeper say to the lord of
the manor?
'The pheasants are revolting'!

What is the definition of Robin?
A bird who steals!

What is a bear's favorite drink?
Koka-Koala!

What do you get if you cross a woodpecker
with a carrier pigeon?
A bird who knocks before delivering
its message!

Where do birds meet for coffee?
In a nest-cafe!

How does a bird with a broken wing manage
to land safely?
With it's sparrowchute!

What is green and pecks on trees?
Woody Wood Pickle!

What happened when the owl lost his voice?
He didn't give a hoot!

What do you call a Scottish parrot?
A Macaw!

What happens when a hen eats gunpowder?
She lays hand gren-eggs!

How do you know if you cat's got a bad cold?
He has cat-arrh!
What is cleverer than a talking cat?
A spelling bee!

How do you know that cats are sensitive
creatures?
They never cry over spilt milk!

What do you get if you cross a cat and a gorilla?
An animal that puts you out a night!

What do you get if you cross a tiger with a kangeroo?
A stripey jumper!

What do you get if you cross a cat with a bottle of vinegar?
A sourpuss!

Why did the owl, owl?
Because the woodpecker would peck 'er!

How are tigers like sergeants in the army?
They both wear stripes!

What do you call a bird that lives underground?
A mynah bird!

What do you call a cat that has just eaten a whole duck?
A duck filled fatty puss!

What kind of animal should you never play
cards with?
A cheetah.

Why do cats chase birds?
For a lark!

What do cats read in the morning?
Mewspapers!

What works in a circus, walks a tightrope
and has claws?
An acrocat!

Why did the cat frown when she passed the
hen house?
Because she heard fowl language!

There were four cats in a boat, one jumped
out. How many were left?
None. They were all copy cats!

Why did the rooster run away?
He was chicken!

What do chickens grow on?
Eggplants!

Why did the chicken cross the basketball court?
He heard the referee calling fowls

What do you get when you cross a chicken with a duck?
A bird that lays down!

Why did the chicken cross the "net"?
It wanted to get to the other site!

What do you get if you cross a parrot with a centipede?
A great walkie-talkie!

What do you call a rooster who wakes you up at the same time every morning?
An alarm cluck!

Why did the chicken cross the road half way?
He wanted to lay it on the line!

Which day of the week do chickens hate most?
Fry-day!

What happens when you drop a hand gren-egg?
It eggs-plodes!

Why did the chick disappoint his mother?
He wasn't what he was cracked up to be!

Is chicken soup good for your health?
Not if you're the chicken!

Why did the chicken cross the road?
To get to the other side!

What did one chicken say to the other after they walked through poison ivy?
"You scratch my beak and I'll scratch yours!"

Why do eskimos do their laundry in Tide?
Because it's too cold out-tide!

Why did the chicken cross the playground?
To get to the other slide!

Why do you need a licence for a dog and not
for a cat?
Cats can't drive!

What do you call a dog in the middle of a
muddy road?
A mutt in a rut!

What do you get if you cross a dog with a
blind mole?
A dog that keeps barking up the
wrong tree!

What do you call a happy Lassie?
A jolly collie!

What do you call a nutty dog in Australia?
A dingo-ling!

What dog loves to take bubble baths?
A shampoodle!

How do you catch a runaway dog?
Hide behind a tree and make a noise
like a bone!

Why don't chickens like people?
They beat eggs!

What dogs are best for sending telegrams?
Wire haired terriers!!

What kind of dog does a vampire prefer?
Any kind of bloodhound!
What kind of dog sniffs out new flowers?
A bud hound!

What happens to a dog that keeps eating
bits off of the table?
He gets splinters in his mouth!

What kind of dog chases anything red?
A bull dog!

What kind of dog wears a uniform and
medals?
A guard dog!

What do you call a dog in jeans and a sweater?
A plain clothes police dog!

What do you get if you cross a dog and a skunk?
Rid of the dog!

What do you get if you cross a computer and a Rottweiller?
A computer with a lot of bites!

What do you get if you cross a dog with a kangaroo?
A dog that has somewhere to put its own lead!

What do you get if you cross a dog and a sheep?
A sheep that can round itself up!

What's big and grey with horns?
An elephant marching band!

What kind of shoes does a mouse wear?
Squeekers

What's big, grey and flies straight up?
An elecopter!

What's grey and never needs ironing?
A drip dry elephant!

What's big and grey and red?
A sunburnt elephant!

What's grey, carries a bunch of flowers and cheers you up when your ill?
A get wellephant!

What did the hotel manager say to the elephant that couldn't pay his bill?
"Pack your trunk and clear out!"

How do you get an elephant into a matchbox?
Take all the matches out first!

What weighs 4 tons and is bright red?
An elephant holding its breath!

Why don't elephants like playing cards in the jungle?
Because of all the cheetahs!

What do you call an elephant with a carrot in each ear?
Anything you want because he can't hear you!

What kind of bird lays electric eggs?
A battery hen!

Teacher: "Which family does the elephant belong to?"
Student: "I don't know! Nobody I know owns one!"

Why did the bull rush?
Because it saw the cow slip!

What do you call an arctic cow?
An eskimoo!

What do you get if you cross a chicken with a cement mixer?
A brick-layer!

How do you fit more pigs on your farm?
Build a sty-scraper!

Why does a rooster watch TV?
For hentertainment!

What do you get from a drunk chicken?
Scotch eggs!

What do you call a crate of ducks?
A box of quackers!

What do you get if you cross a chicken with a bell?
A bird that has to wring its own neck!

What would happen if bulls could fly?
You would have to carry an umbrella all the time and beef would go up!

What do you get if a sheep walks under a cloud?
A sheep that's under the weather!

Why do cows like being told jokes?
Because they like being amoosed!

What do you get if you cross a pile of mud
with a pig?
A groundhog!

How do you take a pig to hospital?
By hambulance!

What do you call a joke book for chickens?
A yolk book!

What do you call a elephant that never
showers?
A smellyphant!

Where does a woodsman keep his pigs?
In a hog cabin!

What is the slowest racehorse in the world?
A clotheshorse!

Why do pigs never recover from illness?
Because you have to kill them
before you cure them!

What do you call a pig who's been arrested
for dangerous driving?
A road hog!

What do you call sheep that live together?
Pen friends!

What do you call a chicken in a shellsuit?
An egg!

How do you start an insect race?
One, two, flea - go!

What is the easiest way to count a herd of
cattle?
Use a cowculator!

What did the baby chick say when he saw
his mother sitting on an orange?
'Dad, dad, look what marma-laid'!

What fish goes up the river at 100mph?
A motor pike!

How could the dolphin afford to buy a house?
He prawned everything!

What kind of fish is useful in freezing
weather?
Skate!

What do you call a fish with no eyes?
Fsh!

What lives in the ocean, is grouchy and hates
neighbours?
A hermit crab!

What do you get from a bad-tempered
shark?
As far away as possible!

Why did the whale cross the road?
To get to the other tide!

What is the most faithful insect?
A flea, once they find someone they
like they stick to them!

What insect runs away from everything?
A flee!

What is the difference between a flea and a wolf?
One prowls on the hairy and the other howls on the prairie!

What to you call a Russian flea?
A Moscow-ito!

What do you call a flea that lives in an idiots ear?
A space invader!

What do you get if you cross a rabbit and a flea?
Bugs Bunny!

How do you find where a flea has bitten you?
Start from scratch!

What is a flea's favorite book?
The itch-hikers guide to humans!

How do fireflies start a race?
Ready steady glow!

How do you keep flies out of the kitchen?
Put a pile of manure in the living room!

What did one firefly say to the other?
Got to glow now!

What goes "snap, crackle and pop"?
A firefly with a short circuit!

Which fly makes films?
Stephen Speilbug!

Why did the firefly keep stealing things?
He was light fingered!

Why were the flies playing football in saucer?
They where playing for the cup!

What is the difference between a fly and a bird?
A bird can fly but a fly can't bird!

Why did the fly fly?
Because the spider spied 'er!

Where would you put an injured insect?
In an antbulance!

What's an insects best chat up line?
Pardon me, but is this stool taken!

What has four wheels and flies?
A rubbish bin!

What happened to the man who turned into
an insect?
He just beetled off!

What is green and brown, has four legs and
can kill you if it falls out of a tree and lands
on you?
A pool table?

How do we know that insects are so clever?
Because they always know when
you're eating outside!

What has 6 legs, bits and talks in code?
A morese-quito!

What is the difference between a mosquito
and a fly?
Try sewing buttons on a mosquito!

What do you get if you cross the Lone
Ranger with an insect?
The Masked-quito!

What has antlers and sucks blood?
A moose-quito!

What is a mosquito's favorite sport?
Skin-diving!

What's the biggest moth in the world?
A mammoth!

What are crisp, like milk and go 'eek, eek, eek'
when you eat them?
Mice Krispies!

What is small, furry and brilliant at sword
fights?
A mouseketeer!

Burhan Siddiqui

What do you get if you try to cross a mouse with a skunk?
Dirty looks from the mouse!

What is a mouse's favorite record?
'Please cheese me'!

What goes eek, eek, bang?
A mouse in a minefield!

What squeaks as it solves crimes?
Miami mice!

What do Scottish toads play?
Hop-scotch!

What did Tom get when he locked Jerry in the freezer?
Mice cubes!

What's gray, squeaky and hangs around in caves?
Stalagmice!

What mouse was a Roman emperor?
Julius Cheeser!

What's a frogs favorite game?
It's croak-et!

What do headmasters and bullfrogs have in
common?
Both have big heads that consist
mostly of mouth!

What powerful reptile is found in the Sydney
opera house?
The Lizard of Oz!

What's the definition of a nervous
breakdown?
A chameleon on a tartan rug!

How do birds make sure their eggs are fine?
They eggsamine them!

Why did the tadpole feel lonely?
Because he was newt to the area!

Where do frogs keep their treasure?
In a croak of gold at the end of the
rainbow!

What's white on the outside, green on the inside and comes with relish and onions?
A hot frog!

What did the bus conductor ay to the frog?
Hop on!

What goes dot-dot-croak, dot-dash-croak?
Morse toad!

Wha'ts the world weakest animal?
A toad, he croaks if you even touch him!

How do you make a glow worm happy?
Cut off his tail, he'll be de-lighted!

What kind of pole is short and floppy?
A tadpole!

What do you call a girl with a frog in her hair?
Lily!

What are spiders webs good for?
Spiders!

Why did the spider buy a car?
So he could take it out for a spin!

What did the worm say to the other when
he was late home?
Where in earth have you been!

When should you stop for a glow worm?
When he has a red light!

What do golfers use in China?
China tees!

What language do they speak in Cuba?
Cubic!

Why did the stupid racing driver make ten
pitstops during the race?
He was asking for directions!

How many balls of string would it take to
reach the moon?
Just one if it's long enough!

What do elves do after school?
Gnomework!

How do we know that the Earth won't come
to an end?
Because it's round!

Where do tadpoles change?
In a croakroom!

What animals are on legal documents?
Seals!

What kind of hair do oceans have?
Wavy!

How do crazy people go through the forest?
They take the psycho path.

How can you tell which end of a worm is
which?
Tickle it in the middle and see which
end laughs!

What kind of lions are in the park?
Dandelions

Friend 1: "What do you mean by telling everyone that I'm an idiot?"
Friend 2: "I'm sorry; I didn't know it was supposed to be a secret!"

Why are goldfish red?
The water turns them rusty!

Why do birds fly south in the winter?
Because it's too far to walk!

Did you hear about the little boy that they named after his father?
They called him dad!

What has forty feet and sings?
The school choir!

What happens when you throw a green stone in the red sea?
It gets wet!

Why did the woman take a loaf of bread to bed with her?
To feed her nightmare!

What city cheats at exams?
Peking!

What makes the leaning Tower of Pisa lean?
It doesn't eat much!

Did you hear about the mad scientist who
put dynamite in his fridge?
They say it blew his cool!

Where does success come before work?
In the dictionary!

How did the telephones get married?
With a couple of rings.

What town in England makes terrible
sandwiches?
Oldham!

What is it that even the most careful
person overlooks?
His nose!

What is a volcano?
A mountain with hiccups!

Why was the broom late?
It over swept!

What runs but never walks?
Water!

Why did the man put his money in the freezer?
He wanted cold hard cash!

Where do bees go to the bathroom?
At the BP station!

What did the porcupine say to the cactus?
"Is that you mommy?"

What do you get when you cross a snowman with a vampire?
Frostbite.

What do prisoners use to call each other?
Cell phones.

Why do leopards have a hard time hiding?
They are always spotted.

Where do snowmen keep their money?
In snow banks.

What's brown and sticky?
A stick.

What do you get when you cross a crocodile
and a camera?
A snapshot.

What dog keeps the best time?
A watch dog.

What did the grape do when it got stepped
on?
It let out a little wine!
How do you make a tissue dance?
Put a little boogey in it!

What did the vampire say about the Dracula
movie?
It was fang-tastic!

What did the water say to the boat?
Nothing, it just waved.

Why don't skeletons fight each other?
They don't have the guts.

When does "B" come after "U"?
When you take some of his honey

What do you call a snowman with a sun tan?
A puddle

What steps would you take if a madman
came rushing at you with a knife?
Really big ones!

How much does it cost a pirate to get
earrings?
A buccaneer
What has four legs and can't walk?
A table

What the same size and shape of an
elephant and weighs nothing?
His shadow

What do you get from nervous cows?
Milk shakes

What do you call a fly when it retires?
A flew

What do you give a dog for a fever?
Mustard, it's the best thing for a
hot dog.

What's black & white and eats like a horse?
A zebra!

What has four legs & sees just as well from
all four sides?
Horse with his eyes shut

Who went into the bear's cave and came out
alive?
The bear

What is bright orange and sounds like a
parrot?
A carrot!

Which side of a chicken has the most feathers?
The outside!

What is the only food that they serve on planes?
Plain food, of course!

Where did the one-legged man work?
I-Hop

What's a ghost's favorite animal?
A cariBOO!

Why did the coach go to the bank?
Because he needed another quarter!

Why did the banana go to the hospital?
Because it was not peeling well!

What do you call a room that does not have walls?
A mushroom.

What's full of holes and still holds water?
A sponge.

Why should you learn sign language?
It's pretty handy!

What did the lettuce say to the tomato while
they were racing?
Hey tomato, ketchup!

What award did the person who invented the
doorknocker win?
The "no-bell" prize.

What is Beethoven doing right now?
De-composing.

What goes "peck, bang, peck, bang, peck,
bang?"
A bunch of chickens in a field full
of balloons!

What does a clock do when it's still hungry?
Go back four seconds!

Which US states has the smallest soft
drinks?
Minisoda.

What did Dr. Dre say to 50 Cent after he gave him a sweater?
Gee, you knit?

What did the grape say when the elephant walked on it?
Nothing. It just gave a little wine.

What's brown and sticky?
A stick.

What did one wall say to the other wall?
Meet you in the corner.

What did the mayonnaise say to the refrigerator?
"Close the door, I'm dressing!"

Why was the baby ant so confused?
Because all of his uncles were ants!

Why does a chicken coop have 2 doors?
Because if it had 4 doors, it'd be a chicken sedan!

Where can you find Mozambique?
On a mozam-bird.

What do you call a fly with no wings?
A walk.

Why did Beethoven get rid of his chickens?
They kept saying "Bach, bach!"

What do you call an alligator in a vest?
An investigator.

Did you hear about what that new pirate
movie was rated?
Arrrrrrr.
How many psychiatrists does it take to
change a light bulb?
Just one - but the light bulb has to
really want to change.

What will mailman man Joe be called when
he retires?
Joe.

Where do sheep get their hair cut?
At the "bah-bah shop."

Why did the man get fired from his job at the orange juice factory?
He couldn't concentrate.

A man walks into a bar and says ouch.
It was a steel bar.

What is the difference between a nicely dressed man on a tricycle and a poorly dressed man on a bicycle?
A tire

What type of an animal needs oil?
A mouse, because it squeaks.

How do you make fruit punch?
You give it boxing lessons.

How do you make seven an even number?
The letter "S" out of it.

Why is a dog like a wedding?
They both need a groom.

What did the blanket say to the bed?
"Don't worry, I've got you covered!"

Why do some football players never sweat?
Because of all their fans!

Why did the one-handed man cross the road?
To get to the second-hand shop.

Why did the turkey cross the road?
Because he wasn't a chicken.

Why did Mickey mouse go to outer space?
He wanted to see Pluto.

Who keeps the ocean clean?
The mermaid.

What did the plant do in math class?
It grew square roots.

Why did Tigger look inside the toilet?
He was looking for Pooh.

What kind of phone does the ocean have?
A shell-phone.

Why didn't the clam share its peals?
It was shellfish.

Where does a turtle go when it's raining?
A shell-ter.

Why did the little bat brush its teeth?
It had bat breath!

What's cute and fuzzy and lives at the
North Pole?
A teddy brrrr.

What happen when the two clumsy oxen
bumped into each other?
They had an oxidant.

What's yellow, comes from Peru, and is
completely unknown?
Waterloo Bear, Paddington Bear's
forgotten cousin!

What is green and brown and crawls through
the grass?
A Girl Scout who has lost her cookie.

Why did the kid study in the airplane?
Because he wanted a higher
education!

Why did the chicken cross the road, roll in
the mud and cross the road again?
Because he was a dirty double-
crosser!

What's yellow on the outside and grey on the
inside?
An elephant disguised as a banana!

What do you get when you cross an
elephant with a fish?
Swimming trunks

Burhan Siddiqui

# Knock Knock Knock Jokes

Knock knock!

Who's there?
Cash.
Cash who?
No thanks, but I would like a peanut instead!

Knock knock!
Who's there?
Doris.
Doris who?
Doris locked, that's why I'm knocking!

Knock knock!
Who's there?
Honey bee.
Honey bee who?
Honey bee a dear and stop knocking!

Knock knock!
Who's there?
Cows go.
Cows go who?
No, cows go moo!

Knock knock!
Who's there?
Oink oink.
Oink oink who?
Make up your mind, are you a pig or an owl?
Knock Knock !

Who's there!
Ice cream!
Ice cream who?
Ice cream if you don't let me in!

Knock Knock!
Who's there?
Urine
Urine Who?
URINEsecure, don't know what for...

Knock Knock!
Who's there?
Wendy.
Wendy who?
Wendy wind blows de cradle will rock.

Knock Knock!
Who's there?
Water.
Water who?
Water you doing in my house?

Knock Knock!
Who's there?
Isabelle.
Isabelle who?
Isabelle necessary on the door?
Knock Knock!

Who's there?
Robin.
Robin who?
Robin your house!

Knock Knock!
Who's there?
Pasture.
Pasture who?
Pasture bedtime isn't it?

Knock Knock!
Who's there?
Cargo.
Cargo who?
Cargo honk, honk!

Knock Knock!
Who's there?
Yule.
Yule who?
Yule never know!

Knock knock
Who's there?
Mikey!
Mikey who?
Mikey doesn't fit in the keyhole!
Knock knock

Who's there?
Howard!
Howard who?
Howard I know?

Knock knock
Who's there?
Beets!
Beets who?
Beets me!

Knock knock
Who's there?
Ice cream!
Ice cream who?
Ice cream if you don't let me in!

Knock knock
Who's there?
Cows!
Cows who?
Cows go 'moo' not who!

Knock knock
Who's there?
Ach
Ach who?
Bless you!
Knock knock

Who's there?
Tank!
Tank who?
You're welcome!

Knock knock
Who's there?
Luke!
Luke who?
Luke through the keyhole and you can see!

Knock knock
Who's there?
Frank!
Frank who?
Frank you for being my friend!

Knock knock
Who's there?
Wooden shoe!
Wooden shoe who?
Wooden shoe like to hear another joke?

# One Liners & Puns

Teacher: "Hivda, give me a sentence using the word, 'geometry.'"
Hivda: "A little acorn grew and grew until it finally awoke one day and said, 'Gee, I'm a tree.'"

I wanted to lose weight so I went to the paint store. I heard I could get thinner there.

I saw a kidnapping today. I decided not to wake him up.

My friend broke her finger today, but on the other hand she was completely fine.

Cartoonist found dead in home. Details are sketchy.

I've been to the dentist several times so I know the drill.

The magician got so mad he pulled his hare out.

I went to the store to buy some soup but they were out of stock.

He didn't tell his mother that he ate some glue. His lips were sealed.

A boiled egg in the morning is hard to beat.

The best way to communicate with a fish is to drop them a line.

The coffee tasted like mud because it was ground a couple of minutes ago.

I should have been sad when my flashlight batteries died, but I was delighted.

The two guys caught drinking battery acid will soon be charged.

I don't think I need a spine. It's holding me back.

A thief who stole a calendar got twelve months.

I used to be a watchmaker. It was a great job and I made my own hours.

In a recession, the most secure job is garbage-man. Business is always picking up.

When the TV repairman got married the reception was excellent.

Math teachers have lots of problems.

I used to be a tap dancer until I fell in the sink.

The comedian stopped at the fabric store on his way to a comedy gig. He was looking for new material.

I probably have blind spots, but I don't see them.

I used to be a banker but I lost interest.

Never lie to an x-ray technician. They can see right through you.

If a judge loves the sound of his own voice, expect a long sentence.

In the room the curtains were drawn, but the rest of the furniture was real.

When an actress saw her first strands of gray hair she thought she'd dye.

Organ donors really put their heart into it.

A guy became so good with a chainsaw that he was promoted to branch manager.

Is it good if a vacuum really sucks?

I heard some hipsters were drowning. They must've fallen into the mainstream.

I tried to catch some fog earlier. I mist

My new theory on inertia doesn't seem to be gaining momentum.

I usually take steps to avoid elevators.

The dead batteries were given out free of charge.

Pencils could be made with erasers at both ends, but what would be the point?

Two peanuts were walking in a tough neighborhood and one of them was a-salted.

Two hats were hanging on a hat rack in the hallway. One hat says to the other, 'You stay here; I'll go on a head."

If you step onto a plane and recognize a friend of yours named Jack don't yell out Hi Jack!

Why can't Cinderella play soccer? She always runs away from the ball!

The doctor told me I had type A blood. I think it was a type O.

I wouldn't want a job crushing pop cans. It's soda pressing.

Did you hear about the guy whose whole left side was cut off? He's all right now.

Aleena wondered why the baseball was getting bigger. Then it hit her.

I'm reading a book about anti-gravity. It's impossible to put down.

I couldn't quite remember how to throw a boomerang, but eventually it came back to me.

I used to have a fear of hurdles, but I got over it.

Did you hear about the guy who got hit in the head with a can of soda? He was lucky it was a soft drink.

Police were called to a daycare where a three-year-old was resisting a rest.

He drove his expensive car into a tree and found out how the Mercedes bends.

I was going to look for my missing watch, but I could never find the time.

The capacitor kissed the diode because he just couldn't resistor.

I try wearing tight jeans, but I can never pull it off.

A prisoner's favorite punctuation mark is the period. It marks the end of his sentence.

I used to be addicted to soap, but I'm clean now.

I was going to buy a book on phobias, but I was afraid it wouldn't help me.

Some people's noses and feet are built backwards: their feet smell and their noses run.

Einstein developed a theory about space, and it was about time too.

I don't trust atoms. They make up everything!

Hey, I love u! It's my favorite vowel.

A book fell on my head and I only have my shelf to blame.
I moustache you a question but I'll shave it for later.

You have cat to be kitten be right meow.

Did you hear about those new reversible jackets? I really want to see how they turn out!

The other day I went to buy some camouflage pants but I couldn't seem to find any.

Did you hear about the scarecrow that won the Nobel Prize for being outstanding in its field?

Burhan Siddiqui

Well we've come to the end of this amazing journey and it really is a shame, isn't it. After all that we've been through, all of the laughs, tears (from laughing that is), and all of the moments where you laughed so hard that no sound came out and you looked like you needed a doctor. But for that, I apologize. I really did have a great time writing this book and compiling these jokes and I would like to thank everyone who helped with this. I'd like to think that this book put a smile on everyone's face and the thought of that is an amazing accomplishment on it's own.

Until the next, stay punny!

Yours,

Burhan Siddiqui

30973944R00074

Made in the USA
Lexington, KY
25 March 2014